Growing Your Child's Spiritual Garden

By Andreah Davi Werner

Illustration By,
Diane Rose Cacioppo

Order this book online at www.trafford.com
or email orders@trafford.com

Most Trafford titles are also available at major online book retailers.

Illustration By: Diane Rose Cacioppo

Printed in the United States of America.

ISBN: 978-1-4669-0550-4

Library of Congress Control Number: 2011962027

Trafford rev. 03/07/2012

   www.trafford.com

North America & international
toll-free: 1 888 232 4444 (USA & Canada)
phone: 250 383 6864 ♦ fax: 812 355 4082

Growing Your Child's Spiritual Garden

Dedication

This book is dedicated to Ian, my first born Grandson,
one of my greatest inspirations in writing and creating our stories.
Ian worked many hours with me in our garden, building shade covers, preparing the soil,
planting seeds, lovingly, watering and nurturing the garden throughout the seasons.
To my adorable, nephews and niece, Adam, Matan and Ranit.
It was Adam who insisted that another garden be
planted like we did when he was a little boy.
Adam especially appreciated spending time with me in the garden,
coming up with ways to build & improve it.
Ranit & Matan, who loved smelling the flowers and singing special songs to them.

To Ylana, who always appreciates the sweetness and beauty of the flowers.
To Nathan, my youngest grandson. When I started
this book he was too little to work in the
garden without attempting to eat the soil. Now Nathan
has also created a beautiful herb
garden. Like his older brother Ian, Nathan loves nurturing his plants.
Many days if you peered into the garden you will hear Nathan,
singing to his plants and saying prayers of thanks to
the Lord for helping his garden to grow.

To my two newest little granddaughters, Adi Aveah and Tova, so little and so precious.
They live in the Holy land of Israel, where there are hundreds of fields filled
with array of colorful flowers throughout the year. Already at such tender young
ages, they also are learning the joys of nurturing and appreciating the garden
To all of the children and adults who will get to experience the joys of
spending time together learning and sharing in their own garden.

"Remember, The Flowers of Tomorrow Are In The Seeds Of Today"

Thanks

With heartfelt gratitude, appreciation and thanks:

To Heather, my beautiful daughter for her support, and creative inserts and editing skills.

To Denny, for helping us with this labor of love, spending many late hours in

post-production bringing the audio and first draft to fruition.

To my Nephew Andrew, with love and belief said; "write your book, don't give up" "JUST DO IT!"

As I worked to complete this book I heard your voice of strength and encouragement.

To my Aunt, "Mora" Dina Feuer & Sylvia Berstein for your love, suggestions,

guidance and support in life and with the writing of this book.

To Diane, my partner in life, who encouraged and assisted me in the creation and

completion of this book. Her drawings helped bring this story into a more

understandable reality for children as well as for the adults who read this book.

It was an enchanting dream like day. Sherra was so proud; she had worked all summer preparing her garden for this day.

Today was the day when her family would come and see and enjoy the beauty of one of GOD's great gifts. How long she had dreamed about this special day.

It was Sunday afternoon; the sun was warm and brightly illuminated the garden. The grass in the garden was so beautiful in some places it actually looked and felt like velvet. It was sometimes hard to tell if it was really real, because it looked so perfect.

Family began to arrive, first her eldest brother Eddy, he was her hero, and he lived very far away. Eddy had to travel a long distance and many days to share this day with his sister. Then some cousins and some younger children entered the gates of the garden.

They all marveled at the uniqueness of colors and different plants. All were in rows next to each other, along the side and in the front of each row a delicate string hung between two small stick like branches, separating the rows from one another as well as protecting the entrance to the newest and most fragile part of the garden.

It was only one week earlier that Sherra's best friend, DiDi had suggested that she collect the branches of a tree that had fallen in last season's storm and use them to hold the dividing string. Sherra remembered how many hours she and DiDi worked scraping all the thorns off the branches, cutting them to make a V shape that would hold the string securely in place.

Looking at them now brought a smile to her face and a feeling of gratefulness for having such a caring and kind friend. She knew that DiDi understood her long time dream to create this garden and was so happy to help her make it happen. Both Sherra and DiDi were feeling proud and appreciated the sense of accomplishment they shared.

Eddy kneeled down to get a closer look at some of the blades of grass that had a blue velvet appearance. He had never seen such colors in a garden before and wanted to be certain that he wasn't being fooled by the planting of a silk plant. As he moved closer to touch and closely look at the unique blue blades, he was over taken with a pleasantly pungent aroma from these mysterious plants. There were so many unusual and beautiful plants as well as some herbs and vegetables too.

Her cousins wanted to know the secrets of the garden. Her cousin Toby was a horticulturist and had actually seen some of these mysterious plants before. But, she had only seen them grow in the rainforests, never before had she seen such an assortment of plants all growing together in a desert environment. Toby was completely baffled, "How did you do it"? she asked. "I mean, I am a horticulturist, I study and grow plants for living, but I have never seen, such a mixture of plants all growing and blossoming like springtime in the fall. How did you do it, what's your secret"?

Sherra replied, "The secret and the answer are both complicated, yet simple. I didn't do it! Sure DiDi and I helped; we planted, watered and fertilized the garden, we even prayed daily for it's growth. But the simple truth is GOD did it. The secrets and mysteries are his, (GOD's). This garden is the Lord's gift to us".

Just then, through the corner of her eye, Sherra saw one of the little cousins climbing over the barrier string into the newest, fragile part of the herb garden. She called out to Sarah, "Wait, don't go there, that part of the garden is not ready for picking it's too young."

To no avail, no sooner had Sherra finished calling to her, when Sarah carelessly stomped on some baby plants. "No, No, Wait"…Too late, Sarah reached down and plucked out two baby garlic bulbs out of the ground.

Sarah was 6 years old and to her;
No, Stop and Wait meant...
Quick, do it before 'No' really counts.
Sherra was furious and immediately
overtaken with anger. Before she knew it
she was yelling and screaming at Sarah.
"You thoughtless, stupid kid, get out of my
garden! How could you do that, don't you
know what you just did"?

Sarah, was stunned, she ran out of the garden crying. Everyone was so surprised to see and hear Sherra behave in such a way. Everyone became quiet and sad. Some of the cousins left the garden. It was as if darkness had fallen over the garden. Even some of the plants began to droop down.

Sherra, realizing what she had just done was instantly filled with sadness and remorse and she too began to cry. "Oh what a mess I've made of this day" Sobbing, "why did I have to react like that? I was so mad, whayhaa" ...Both Sherra and Sarah were crying now. Eddy consoled Sherra, "I can see why and how upset with the situation you are. Yes, you could have handled it in a better way. How about this, I'll go and talk with little Sarah and you stop your crying and think of the way you really would have liked to handle this. What was the outcome you really would have liked to see take place"? Eddy wiped Sherra's tears away and they decided it would be better to walk over to Sarah together.

Sherra and Eddy approached little Sarah who had her face buried in her mother's lap. Sherra knelt down, and gently raised Sarah's chin up. Softly gazing into Sarah's eyes, Sherra apologized for her outrage. "I'm so sorry for yelling at you like that, and calling you stupid. That was a terrible thing to say. You're not stupid and I am so sorry for hurting your feelings like that. I was just so upset with you. I should have handled it differently. Please won't you give me another chance to show you why I was so upset"? Sarah wiped her tears and looked up into Sherra's eyes, "Cousin Sherra, I'm also sorry. Will you forgive me too"?

"Certainly, won't you come and walk with me back into the garden? I would like to show you something." Sherra took Sarah's hand and together they slowly walked back to the garden. As they walked, Sherra explained all the love and care she and DiDi had put into the planting of their garden and the importance of allowing the herbs and vegetables to mature before picking them.

Sherra took Sarah over to the two gaping holes in the ground from where she had plucked out the baby garlic bulbs. "Look," said Sherra, "look deep into the holes." Sherra shined a small red light into the hole so Sarah could see what was left inside.

"What is that," replied Sarah, "why are those spaghetti like things wiggling all around? They look like they have fur on them, how come? Why did you use a red light instead of a bright flashlight to see in the hole"? "Those are good questions, Sarah. First those wiggly things are the roots. They are wiggling all around because they are alive. They were attached to the garlic bulb feeding it nourishment so it would grow. The fur that you saw on them was a soft hair, called rhizoids."

"They help to capture the moisture and nutrients in the roots to feed to the plants. I used a small red light instead of the bright flashlight so I would not harm the tender roots. They are not ready for the bright lights of the day yet.
They are growing and still too young."

Sarah wanted to fix what she had done. "Now, that I understand better, I am really sorry," she said to Sherra and to the little plant. "Hey, do you think if we put the bulb back into the hole the roots may want to feed the garlic bulb again and make it grow," asked Sarah? "Well, I'm not sure, but it's a possibility. Perhaps if we carefully place the bulbs back in the holes, and add some special vitamins and water along with a special prayer, maybe it will start it grow again."

"It's certainly worth the efforts!" So Sherra and Sarah did just that, they re-planted, watered, fertilized the two plants. Then all together, along with Sarah's Mommy, DiDi and Eddy, they all prayed to GOD and asked for the continued growth of the little garlic bulbs.

Sherra and Sarah decided that they would spend time together once every week, nurturing the special garden, helping it to grow.

Soon the warm sun began to shine and once again all the plants seemed happier. Even the rest of Sherra's family were happier too.

Sherra and Sarah eagerly looked forward to the day when they could harvest some of the garlic and vegetables. They were both very excited and wanted to make some yummy spaghetti sauce and vegetables to share with their friends and family.

51

Eddy was proud of his sister and Sarah for the way they worked out their misunderstandings. Eddy was also proud of the way Sherra and Sarah worked together to create a happier ending and a happy, healthy garden too.

Thank you Lord for the dream, the story and the combination of love that brought this first story to fruition. May it bring togetherness, joy and the ability to create healthier, happier outcomes for all those who read and share this story.

BLESSED BE HE WHO MAKES OUR SPIRTUAL GARDEN GROW.

Todah L 'EL	That is Hebrew for saying (Thank You Lord)
Todah HaShem	That is also Hebrew for saying (Thank You Lord)
Gracias Dios	That is Spanish for saying (Thank You Lord)
Grazie Dio	That is Italian for saying (Thank You Lord)
Kamisama Arigatō	That is Japanise for saying (Thank You Lord)

GLOSSARY OF WORDS

In the order as they appear in the story

1. **SPIRITUAL**: A GOD like special thought

2. **ENCHANTING**: Charming or delightful, a little magical

3. **ILLUMINATED**: To make something Visible or bright with light; To be lit up

4. **UNIQUENESS**: Being only one of its kind; Different then the others in it's own special way

5. **MARVELED**:   To be wowed or very impressed, surprised or amazed

6. **ACCOMPLISHMENT**: To complete or finish something

7. **APPEARANCE:** The way something or someone looks to other people or the other person

8. **PUNGENT AROMA:** A very strong smell or a powerfully sharp bitter taste

9. **MYSTERIOUS**: Something that is not known much about. It may be questionable or hard to explain.

10. **HORTICULTURIST:** A person who studies and grows all sorts of plants

11. **ASSORTMENT:** A group of different items or a variety or mixture of different items

12. **ENVIRONMENT:** What is around you: Nature or your surroundings

13. **BAFFLED:** Not sure, your mind is ,mixed up or confused, puzzled, unsure or uncertain about

14. **COMPLICATED**: Hard or difficult to understand

15. **FERTILIZED**: To give plants special food, and or vitamins to help it grow

16. **BARRIER**: A wall or a fence that separates one place from another

17. **FRAGILE**: Not strong, weak or easy to break

18. **NO AVAIL**: To not pay any attention to; No matter what was said it didn't matter

19. **FURIOUS**: To be very angry

20. **IMMEDIATELY**: Right away, right now, not later

21. **THOUGHTLESS**: Without care. Doing something without thinking about it first

22. **STUNNED:** Surprised, shocked or amazed

23. **REALIZING:** To understand or become aware of something you did or something around you

24. **REMORSE:** Feeling sadness or sorry for something that you may have said or did

25. **WHAYHAA:** Crying sound

26. **CONSOLED:** When someone listens and talks with a person, helping them to understand or feel better

27. **APOLOGIZED:** When someone said they were sorry for what they did or what may have happened

28. **OUTRAGE:** To cry or yell out in anger

29. **CERTAINLY:**   To know for sure, without a question in your mind

30. **MATURE:** To be all grown up or fully developed

31. **GAPING:** To be wide open or very large and open

32. **REPLIED:** Answered

33. **NOURISHMENT:** To give food, drink or vitamins

34. **RHIZOIDS:** A soft hair like furry growth, like what was on the roots of the plant in the story

35. **CAPTURE:**   To catch something

36. **MOISTURE:** Wetness

37. **NUTRIENTS:** Food or vitamins

38. **POSSIBILITY**: Maybe it can happen

39. **NURTURING**: Giving or taking care of something or someone

40. **EAGERLY**:   Ready, and wanting very much to do something

41. **HARVEST**: To pick and gather

42. **MISUNDERSTANDINGS**: To not understand what somebody meant; To have a disagreement or argument

43. **COMBINATION**: To put more than one thing together

44. **FRUITION**: To finally happen; To reach a goal that you have been working towards; To come to completion

45. **OUTCOMES**: The way something turns out; The end result

SUPPORTIVE & CHILD SAFE WEBSITES
helping children to cultivate the love of learning gardening

_____

Listed below are some websites that we believe will be very supportive with your child's gardening efforts. This is another wonderful part of interactive learning that an adult and child can do together. You will also see listed other websites that you can go to find additional gardening tools, seeds and information.

#1   Mom's Homeroom at MSN.com
http://momshomeroom.msn.com/videos/4/234

#2   Garden Tools for Small Hands
http://www.forsmallhands.com   (and search for item # SC628)

#3   How to Guide Kids in Garden Planting.
http://blossombunkhouse.com/2011/06/28/how-to-guide-kids-in-garden-planting

#4   National Junior Horticultural Association.
http://www.njha.org

#5   Plants that move when you tickle them.
http://www.ticklemeplant.com

#6   How to grow ideas for sprouts, simple garden recipes to buying seeds and more
http://www.cooksgarden.com/vegetables/sprout-seed

#7   Another place to buy seeds.
http://burpee.com

#8   More ideas for gardening with children.
http://www.growveg.com/growguides/gardening-with-children.aspx

<u>About the Author</u>

Andreah Davi Werner is an energetic public speaker, has appeared on radio, TV shows and commercials. She has authored three audio books, 'Sweet Momma Reflections', 'Reflections II', 'Grandchildren & Art', 'Growing Your Child's Spiritual Garden' and one poetry book, 'Obsessions of A Winged Heart'. Andreah has published numerous articles on nutrition and lifestyle changes. She holds certifications in Herbal Medicine, Holistic Rehabilitation, Holistic Hypnotherapy, Theta Healing, Emergency Medicine. She is very actively involved with her community, raising funds and awareness for multiple charities. She is a Lion Of Judah and a Woman of Philanthropy. Andreah says, "My most favorite times are spent teaching children creative ways of expression through art, gardening, photography and various creative projects.

The formative years of my life were in Long Island, New York where the grounds were rich with green grass and trees, the soil was fertile and each season had a definitive difference. The air was humid, the forests were lush and the spring and summertime flowers bloomed everywhere.

Continued on next page...

ABOUT THE AUTHOR
Continued

By the age of nine my family & I had moved to Las Vegas, Nevada. The desert was quite the opposite of New York. The rich soil and lush forests were replaced with hard, dry soil, vast hot desert lands full of prickly cactus. Yet after a time, the desert too showed its mystic' and beauty. In the springtime the desert produced an array of colorful flowering cacti. Although there weren't many trees there were some hidden springs and a few oases in the middle of the desert. They were green, lush, refreshing and beautiful. It was then that I realized, with proper nutrients, nourishment and love, a garden could grow even in the middle of the desert.

I believe the same holds true for every person.

I owe much of my life's success first to the credit of the Almighty, and to my loving parents and siblings. My mother always told me I could pretty much do whatever I wanted to do. However in order to achieve it; I had to visualize it, believe in it and in myself. My father taught me the value of proper physical nutrients and nourishments. As well as understanding the value of preparing for the unknown or (*what if this happened) type of planning.* All of this combined with unconditional love and kindness of my parents and siblings, I learned the values of creating winning outcomes. Taking the time to listen, care and to try and understand one another is the nourishment that ultimately blossoms the seeds of our flowers, which are our children. These are just a few of the lessons of the WC Spiritual Garden Book series." Andreah says she wants parents, teachers and children to experience the lessons and joys of creating their own spiritual garden together.

A portion of proceeds from the sale of this book will be donated to the various charities that feed and educate children around the world.

This Package of seeds is our gift to you for being a contributor in part.

To Order Your Free Packet of Spiritual Garden Seeds:

Go to   http://www.wcspiritualgardens.com

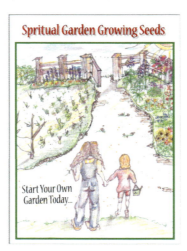

To order an audio version of this book go to:
http://www.wcspiritualgardens.com

*G*rowing Your Child's Spiritual Garden
By Andreah Davi Werner

Illustration By,
Diane Rose Cacioppo

A warm and inspiring story teaching children and adults alike, the lessons of nurturing and respecting one another, with solutions to create positive outcomes experienced through the love and joy of gardening together.

This book encourages adults and children to read together and offers support for the older child who wishes to read independently. It is perfect for children 4 through 10 years of age; pre-school through fourth grade.

A portion of all proceeds from purchase of this book will go to various charitable organizations that help to feed and educate children around the world.
As a special thank you and an incentive to begin a child's spiritual garden, the author has included an offer for a complimentary starter package of 'WC Spiritual Garden Seeds'.

RECEIVE A FREE PACKAGE OF WC SPIRITUAL GARDEN SEEDS
www.wcspiritualgardens.com
This book is also available in audio-book formats

Printed by
EDWARDS BROTHERS
www.edwardsbrothers.com
04SKC12MDJa